The Dust

of Us

The Dust of Us

Poems

By
Michelle Boske

The Dust of Us
Copyright © 2014 by Michelle Boske

This is a fictional collection of poetry. The
events, names, and characters are fictitious,
and any similarity to real persons, living or
dead, or actual events are purely coincidental.

Cover Design:
Ryan Boske-Cox artgal77@yahoo.com

ISBN-10: 1-941938-01-9
ISBN-13: 978-1-941938-01-0

Table of Contents

Dedication

This book is for Kevin. It's also for Connor and Molly.

I can't imagine this crazy, beautiful journey without them.

Their persistent love and support sustains me.

Nobody has ever measured, not even poets, how much the heart can hold.
— Zelda Fitzgerald

Crust of us— dust of us, love spending its life wishing to be whole again.

–Michelle Boske

Cool Like We Used to Be

We hold up walls with our backs
eat runny cheese
off crackers with tiny black seeds
which fall on my blouse

My shoes pinch but
with nowhere to sit—
slick glass seats are
according to the hostess,
stylish modern art pieces
not for sitting

Ice clinks in scotch-filled glasses
a smile plays on our lips
I swirl the merlot
taking small sips
grapey and sweet—
my lips pucker against
a fruity punch

Dumping its contents
into potted plants
realizing entirely too late
it's shredded-paper soil—
the fronds shiny plastic

We snicker low
then lose it
altogether
our bodies doubled-over
in a just can't-help-it
kind of laughter
drawing polite stares
and not-so-kind whispers

So
as dessert is presented
tiny perfect confections
on laden silver trays
we make our way past a bathroom
"just for show"
collect our coats
and into the night
make our escape.

Salt Makes Us

Ocean's edge

wind in hair
            tang of salt

teasing tongues
                reminding us

we're alive
            nothing is ever as big as the sea

our lives
        our love

never as deep or wide
                    or unending

drifting on waves
        you are the tide coming back to me

Slung low on the horizon
                    setting sun lulls us

layers of orange and magenta
                    our blanket

warm sugary sand
            our bed

tiny grains of distant memory
                    our familiar sheen

We allow ourselves
we sink slowly
until
we're buried
beneath a cover
of
hopeless nostalgia
too lazy
to even look
for constellations in the sky.

Milquetoast

I took a detour there,
hung my heart on branches
too high to retrieve
again
misplaced love tried too hard
how were we to know
each other, now love?

Toothpaste globs always
cling too stubbornly
and whiskers coat
the porcelain
please pick up milk
feed the cat
these are some things
I said to him
in a fit of banality
we jest as a way of overcoming

What I meant to say is this,
I would meet you there.
let me mask the indifference
of the world
wrap it in yellow tissue
look at its sunny soul!
secrets doled out

I saw myself
why do some stand and scream
and others just lay down to rest
he pointed out I never did either
I waited while he waxed poetic
about the colors of autumn
but it's spring he loved best

Shhh
sleep now
milk toast
becomes us.

Its Golden Lips

Cold winter morning
snuggled
deep in covers,
my children and I

A magnificent tangle
of arms and legs—
soft bodies, warmed, breathing
together

We've never seen weather like this
wrinkled furious brow
of the grey horizon
beyond our window

I inhale sweet musky scents
kiss silky hair
eyelids flutter but none open

I dare not move
hot breath on my cheeks
small fingers wrapped
around my curls

Reminding me
just once— let the
glossy glow of morning
unfold slowly—
let its fingers reach me

Pour light from its golden lips
diamonds from a velvet pouch
filling in cracks
illuminating darker corners

Our blanket pulled up
against the wet-sheeted sky
sleepy heads, in a row,
gentle ache of love
shining through.

The Dust of Us

I'm still here
just like you knew I'd be
Predictable—
a steady rhythm of
heart beats

Pounding here where you aren't
in this place
that used to be ours
and it's not looking good

Entangled in these goddamned
cocoon threads
holding me in place
but not together

The outside world
rolls in
constant streams
color and light
blurred edges
slipping in and out of humanity

Darkness thickens
the heat clicks on
another day gone

This dryness stretched thin
long suffering fools
with the could haves and
should haves
the might have beens

My head full of you—
bursting at its seams
until doubt and regret
poured
into tiny cracks

Now only broken promises
I've fed
held in my palms
coddled
made real

Loss wedged so deep
into my withered
weakened heart

Until
it simply shatters
scattering tiny particles
of you and me everywhere

The dust of us
will settle into corners
little piles of nothingness
until they're swept up
or forgotten.

Anchor

Thank you
for the coffee—
it's been too long
and you saved me from a day
I'd not wanted to face

Tucked away
in our cozy corner booth
wayward sailors—
adrift on waves of conversation

Wrapping chilled hands,
we unravel days
around these steaming cups
warming me from fingertips
to shivering soul—
It's my life preserver and
I cling to it

Finding solace in this harbor
we both pause
listening to sounds
of life around us—
clank of metal
clinking porcelain
cups and saucers

Whirring grinder
gentle murmur
of hushed voices

This life's business
cannot escape us long—
I wrap up in your words
taking this cover
out into a chilly
rain-soaked day

Thank you for distraction
friend
for coffee and perfect
conversation—

This tiny revelation:

Seeing your smile
and the last foamy
sip of latte—
I'm stronger
I discover,
than I thought.

Birds Know Everything

Pecking away at the ground
I always wonder
if they found something
or if birds are just
optimistic

Just frittering away
trying for scraps of
something
anything
tiny specks of hope
scattered across the universe

A frayed-yarn God's eye
in the window;
our lives strung
along the sill
with jars of rocks—
dry bones of memory
the children dug up

I remember
you would lay my head
on your chest
your heart would thrum gently
beating words just for me
bah-bump only you only you
only you.

These Ghosts

Writers are haunted
by aching ghost teeth
long decayed
with distant memories—
pulling them out
is just another day.

Old is the New

Young

We were young
once—
before time had
its way with us

a youthful gait
loose and free

making love
on lazy Sunday afternoons
lithe bodies and
skin smooth

soft

our hearts
filled with desire
bodies electric
heads thick with purpose
yet always in the clouds

we scattered dreams—like seeds across
earth

our salt over shoulders— let breezes
carry them away

always sowing, never reaping

allowing our drifting souls to
tumble recklessly
across the great expanse
landing wherever we wanted

getting older was a distant thing
tucked away in folds of laundry
later than was possible

But—
time has its way

of

stretching

out

thinning already
threadbare lives
quietly, no ceremony

unraveling plans we made

we are not done yet—
it's not too late, we tell ourselves
a few seeds remain
in our pockets
we know how to tend them
now

we dig in our heels
hold tight
demand the right to our dreams
spiraling us toward a future
we'd not entirely imagined.

.

Exhales

I'm afraid
your eyes— haunting—
they
muddle my mind
thresh my heart
ruin me

never saying enough

what lies beneath
this moment
unspoken,
wanting
drifting
waiting

holding our breath
—the way we do
fearing single exhales
blowing the other away

searching
reaching
you in the dark
I find you here —
no longer an apparition
tangled sheets and
the salt of you
a rind
of you

I would hold your face
drink your soul
if you wanted—
wander the chambers of your heart
chains rattling,
looking for the key

I'd risk it all if—
 you'd
feel pain, too

miss me   crave me

— a ghost limb

Siren's Call

Like fallen silk
water worn stones,
words poured from rosy lips
pressed through fog
the bone chilling treason

resting in my cove
from the cold, a respite.
a glistening mirage
desolation sung out in beats
from enchanted songs

tempting you,
seducing
swallowing you

lapping body
and soul
an incurable languor;
sadness complete

from my rock,
I know you, fighting
against demons,
dive under waves, so deep
sinking into darkness

seeking redemption spun
from a siren's silver tongue
regret is a whisper
drifting on waves

Forty-Three

Birds mark time
better than anyone
beat wings against
coming chill
follow dreams
drink stars from the sky

On a walk with my daughter
filling our pockets with pinecones
October rattling our bones
tucking in scarves

around us

leaves loosen themselves
from anchors—
delicate
paper-thin, curled,
whirling;
a gentle waltz
painting with autumn's hues

Sun sinks low
on the horizon
Standing here
loose
yet not fully unhinged,
still tethered
to all that keeps me
rooted

These dog-eared days
become us
light folds us in two
where else could we be
but here?

I'm as beautiful
as I'm ever
going to be
and when music plays,
I dance.

Distraction

One morning
after a week of storms
the sun punched through clouds
streamed in our windows
casts of unyielding spotlights

We shaded our eyes against
this intrusion
stumbled from bed
toward the kitchen
to grind coffee and make toast

An ordinary table morning
cracked blue leather chairs
my pen scribbling lists
your mind wandering
our thoughts ricocheting
soundly
off pale green walls

Sometimes
when I'm supposed
to be writing
I look out the kitchen window and
watch birds.

Postcards

While you traveled the world
taking blurry photos of yourself
I spent that winter alone
cocooned in endless blankets
revisiting Tolstoy, Atwood,
Kafka

You sent me dimly lit pubs
and sun-baked ruins
unspooling memories meant
just for you

shiny fucking postcards
with brief scrawls
on their backs
Having fun!
Wish you were here!
and the pièce de résistance
Too much rain.

I wrote a poem for you
did you even know
words formed on lost lips
poured from my tongue
fallen desire
dripping onto pages
this keyhole nostalgia
of creamy white stationery

Never thought to ask
maybe telling yourself I didn't care—
I did
but
we were out of words
by then

the silence of distance
sliding
down our throats
thick as honey.

Auld Lang Syne

So much of the year forgotten

things tucked away

friends left uncalled

unwritten poems

on a desk, crumpled lists

for another day

so little is stone

we are always moving

rearranging

rescheduling

redoing

checking off our days

in neat little squares

row after row, Xs, black

long stretches

unremarkable in tiny ways

together
strung beads on thin wire
skim of dust blanketing everything
a slow smelting of hours

that bone-aching betrayal
time plays with us all—
sometimes we hear
the crisp clear sound of
our promises breaking

but listen, too
this sloppy
heartbreaking
utterly beautiful life,
we all have that

some days hope

swells in our chests

rings inside us like a chime

delicate beating music

for our sore, full hearts

we remake our

days ourselves

soaring

we begin again.

Acknowledgments

To Kevin Boske, Stephanie Peterson, Linda Grose, and David Grose. I'm grateful for your enduring support. You were always there to tell me to try, and for that you have my profound thanks and love.

To D.K. Cassidy. Thanks for your guidance and support, and for putting up with my luddite-ness!

To Keith Reimer, unofficial editor extraordinaire. Thank you for being my reader and for all your feedback.

To EJ Runyon, my writing coach and editor. Thank you for sloughing through all the rough drafts to help me find the nuggets, guiding my craft, and encouraging me.

About the Author

Michelle Boske is a former teacher and lifelong writer. She writes poetry and short fiction. She lives in the Pacific Northwest with her husband and two children. While writing, she occasionally drinks too much coffee. When not writing, Michelle enjoys traveling, reading, corny puns, and spicy food.

If you enjoy her work, please follow her at:

facebook.com/author.michelle.boske

twitter.com/glassreallyfull